Taylor the Thankful Turkey

Written by Sonica Ellis

Illustrated by Nejla Shojaie

ISBN 978-1-7372647-3-6

Dear Reader,

Today I'm thankful for you.
Thank you for reading this book. It means
the world to me. I hope you find the story
and message uplifting.

Just remember to always be thankful even
for the little things. Just like my grams
always says gratitude is the best attitude.

Happy Thanksgiving!

Love Always,

DEDICATION:

This book is dedicated to Kathy Seifert
without whom my Thanksgiving dinners
would not have been nearly as tasty!

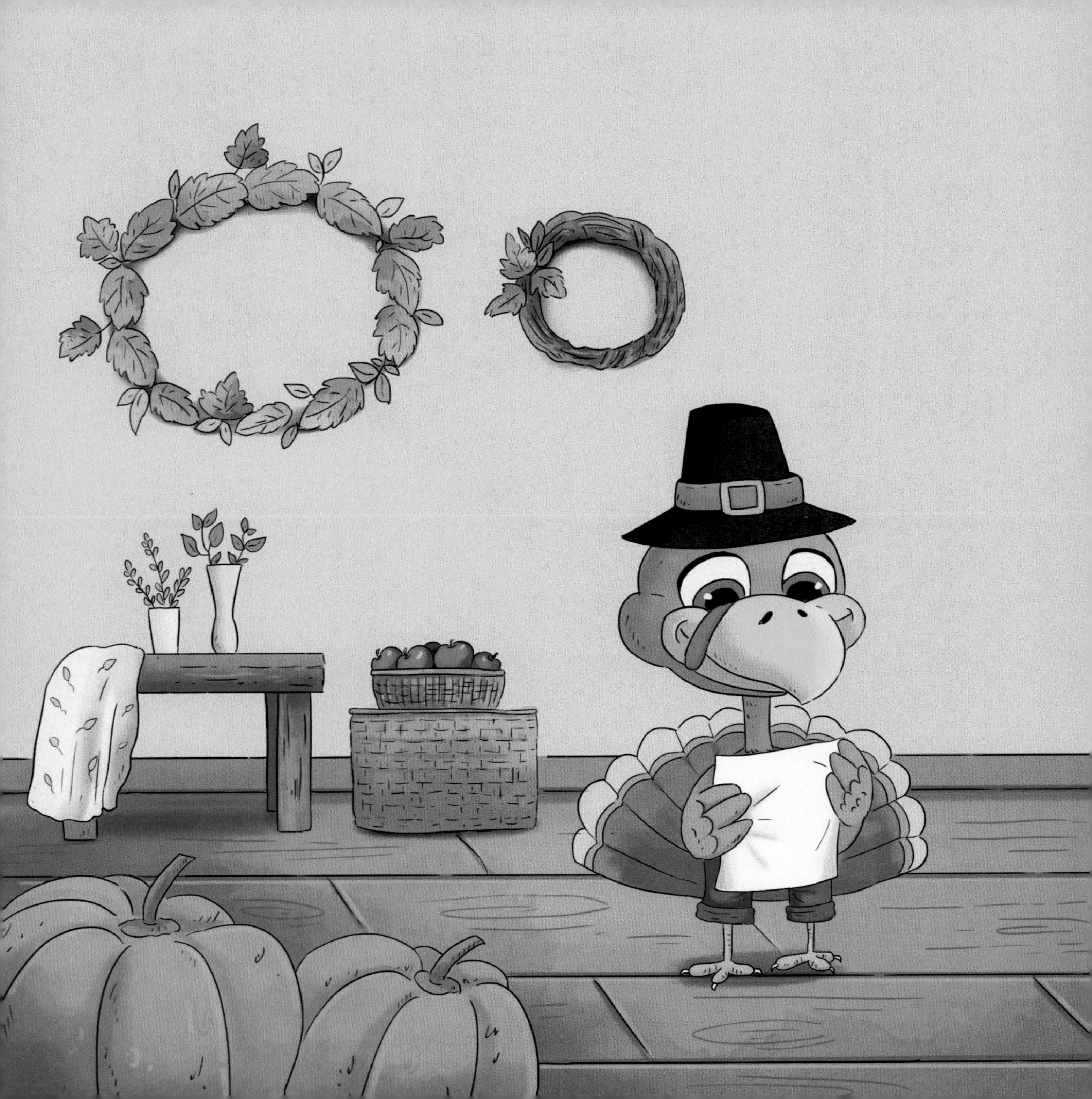

It was Thanksgiving Day in the town of Cranberry Hills and Taylor Turkey was dressed and ready to go.

He had a list of all the houses he needed to visit.

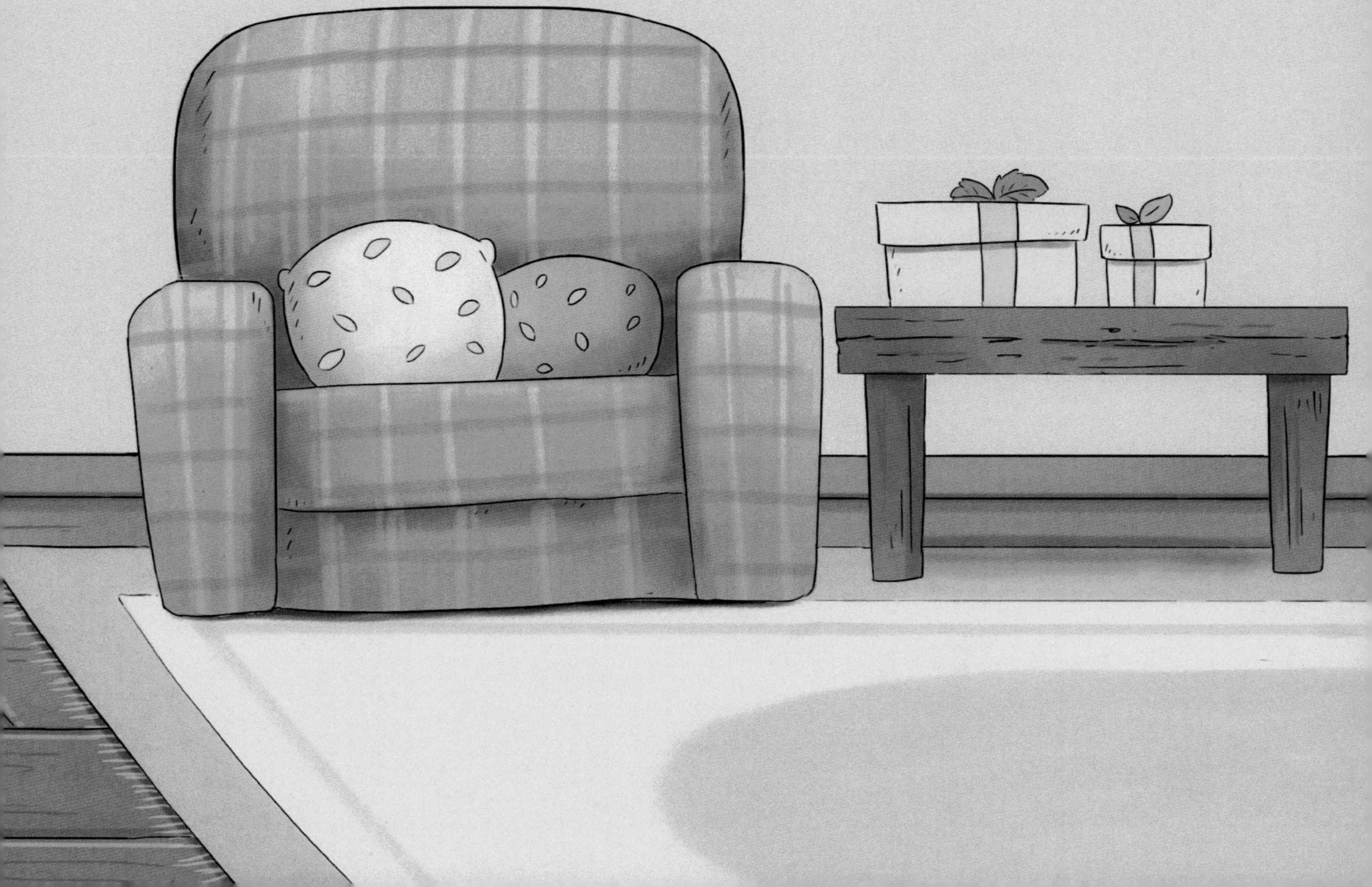

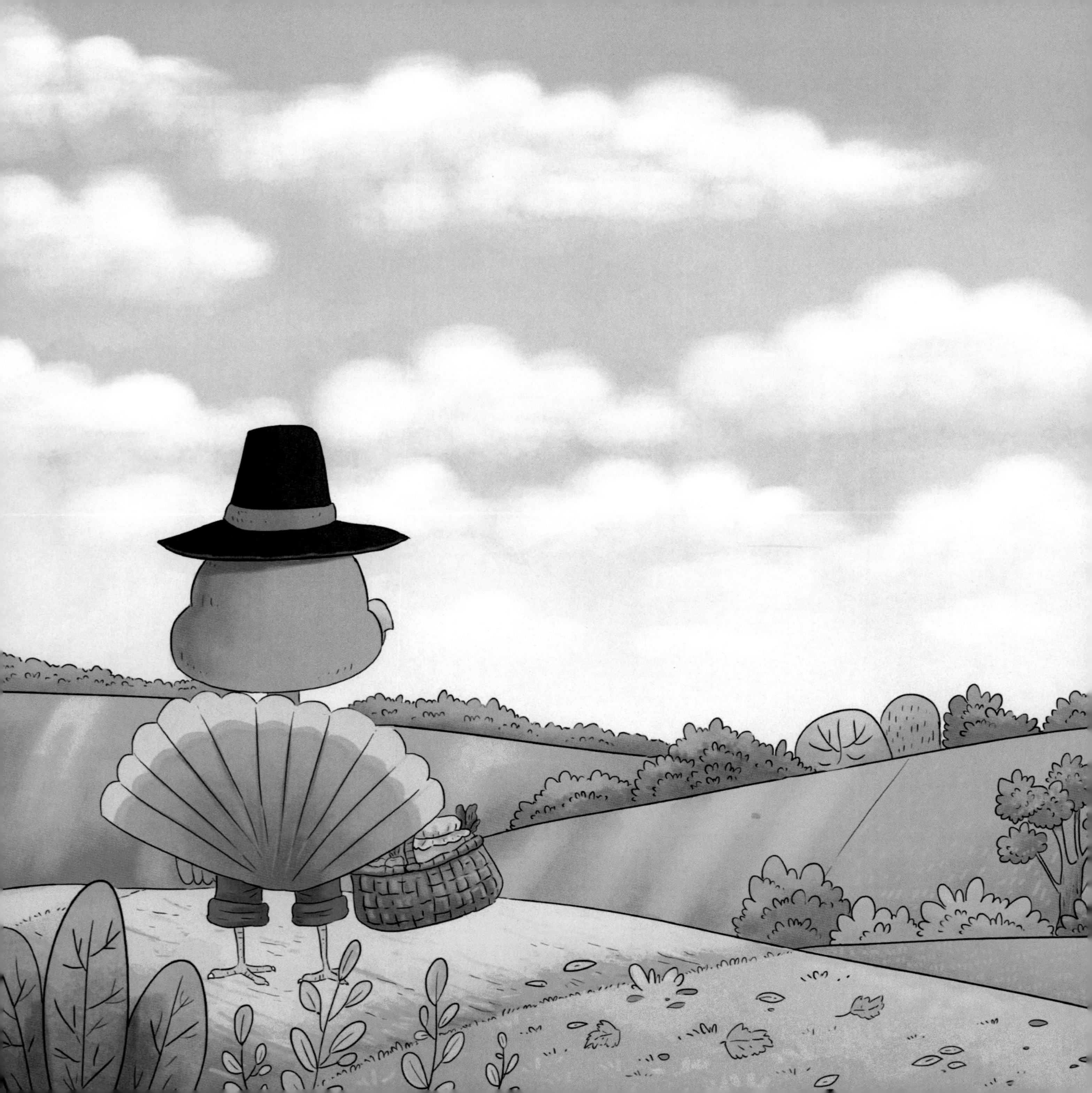

Taylor grabbed his basket of goodies and off he went, down the road to Teddy Bear's house.

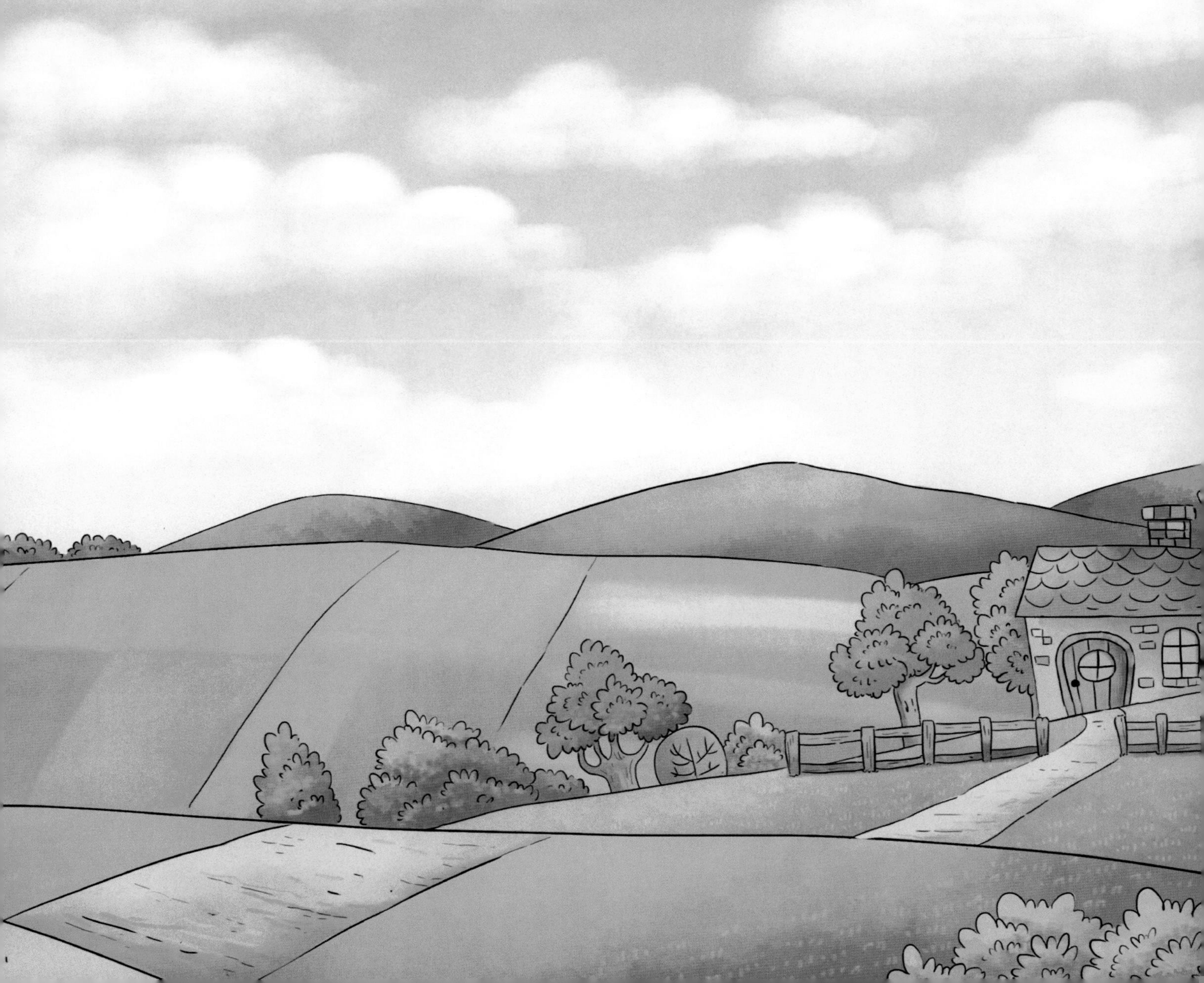

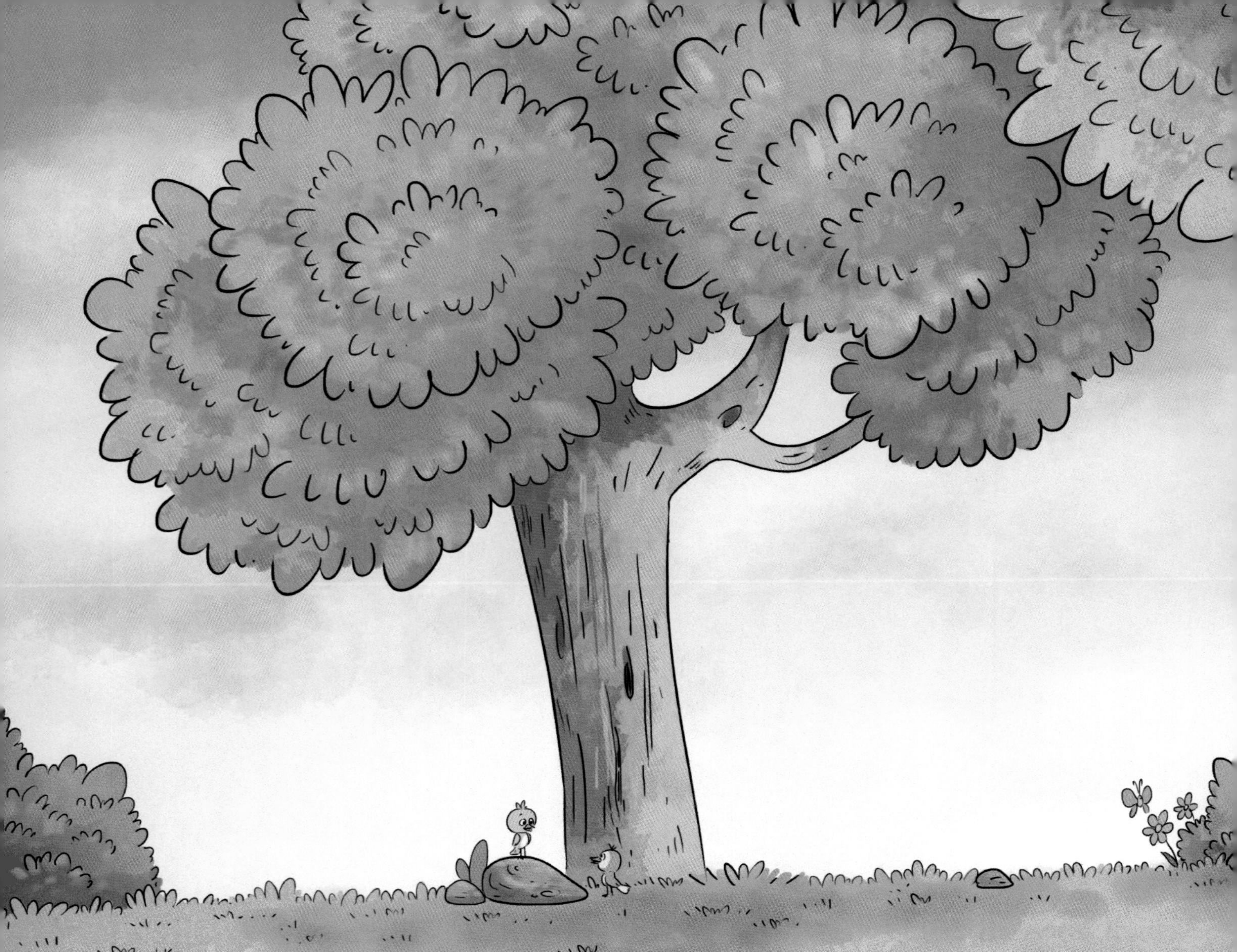

When he arrived, Taylor knocked on the door.
"Hello," Taylor said. "I wanted to let you know that I am thankful for all the things you've done for me.
I would like to give you a jar of sweet homemade honey sauce."

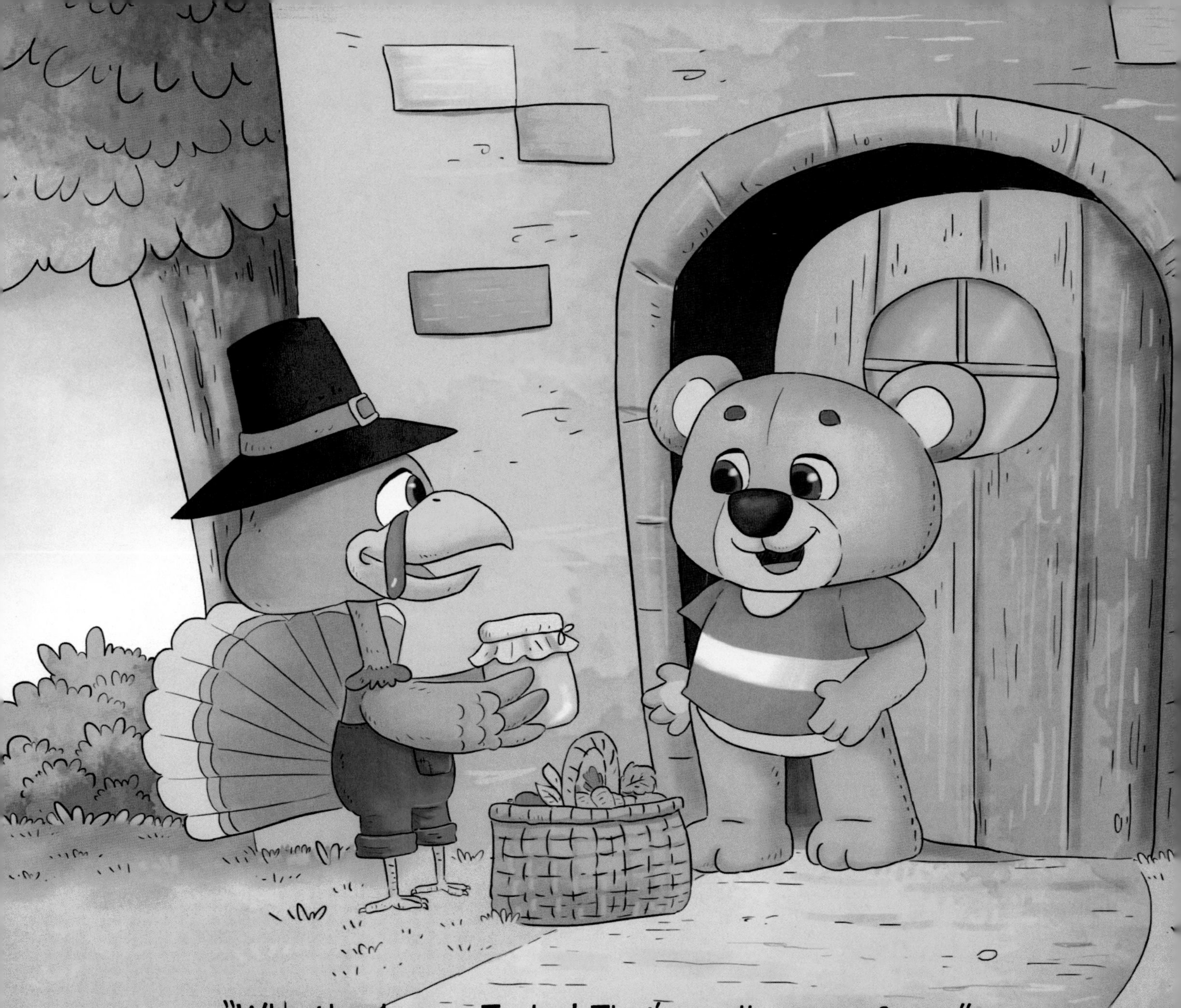

"Why thank you, Taylor! That's really nice of you," Teddy replied. "I hope you have a great Thanksgiving."

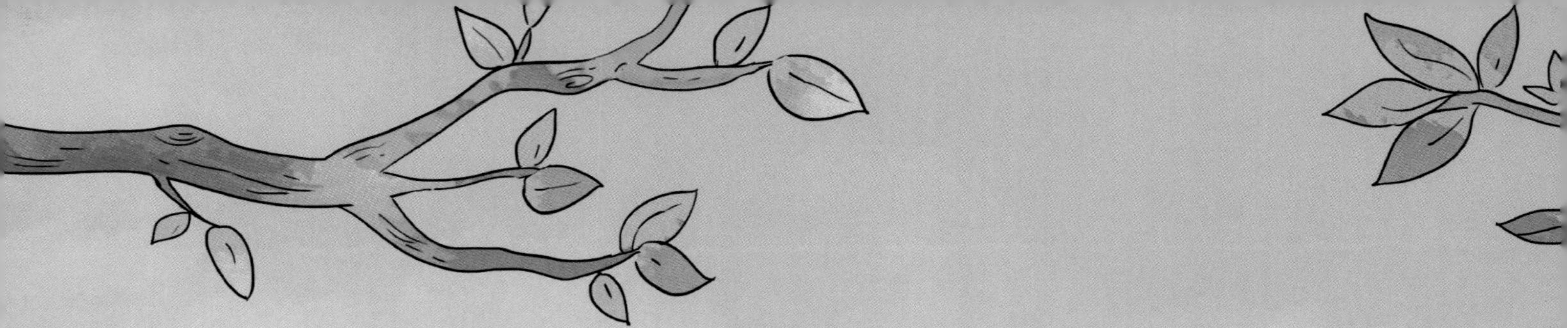

Taylor hurried to the next house on his list.
Once again, he knocked on the door.

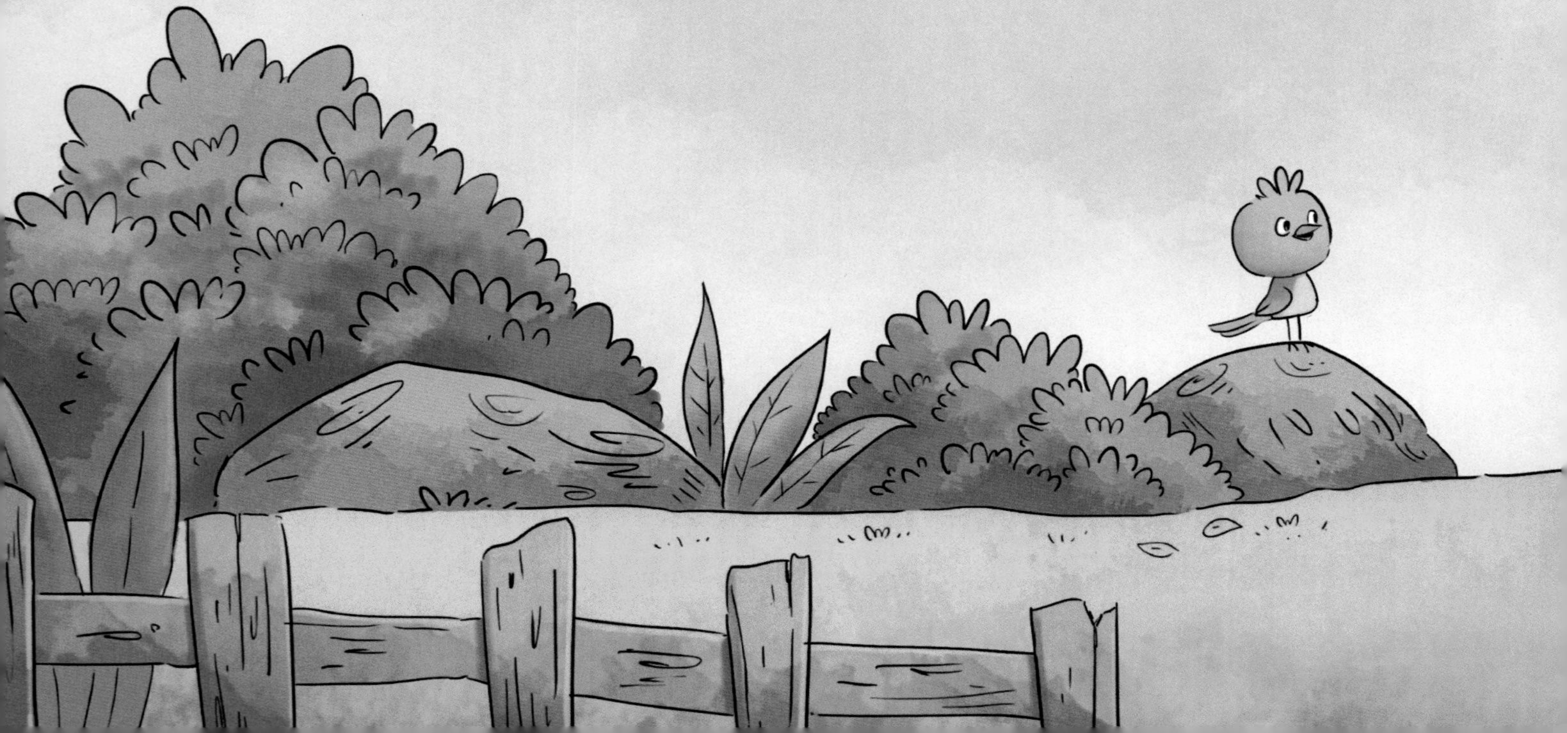

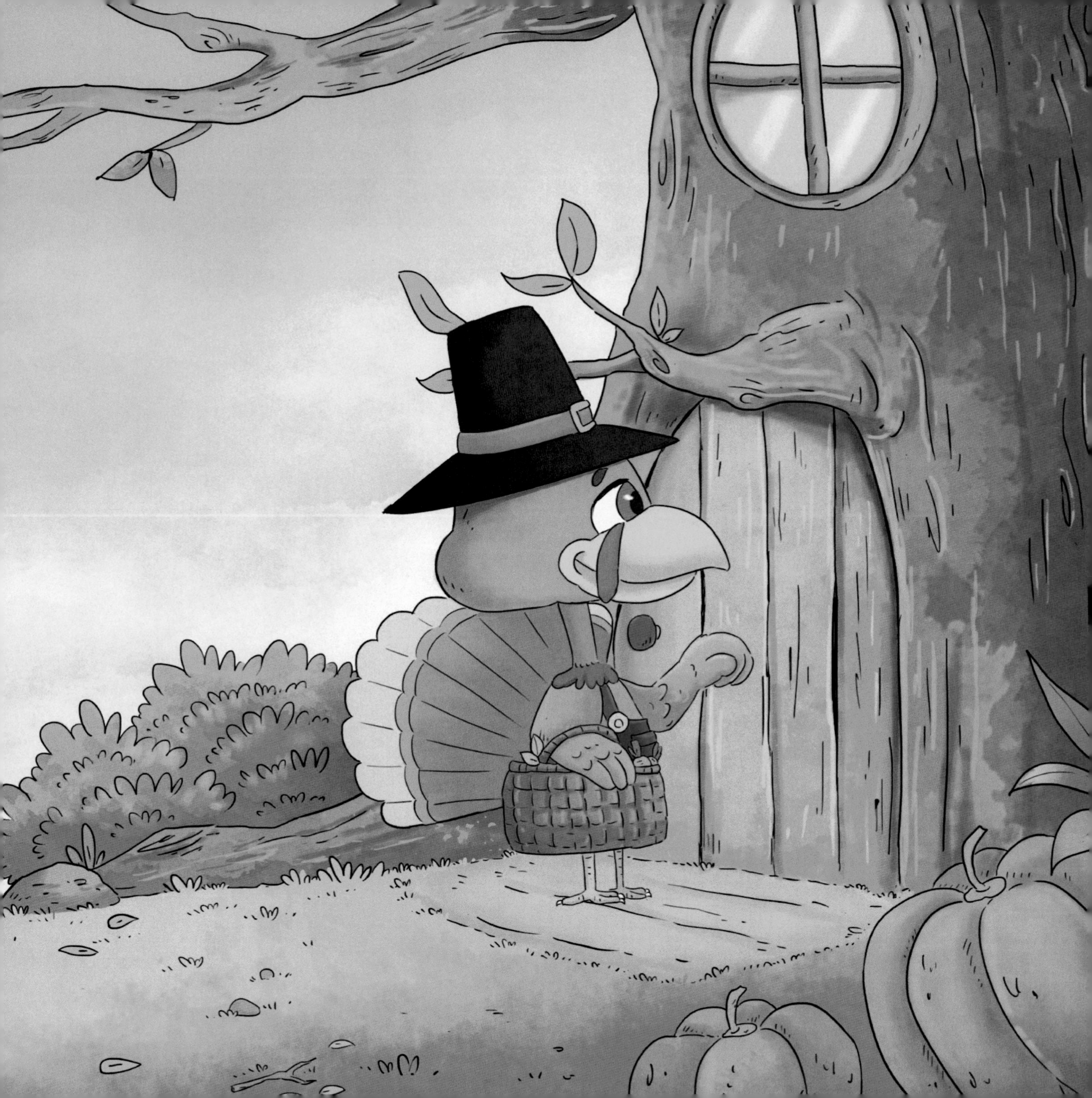

This time, Mrs. Squirrel answered.
"Hello, Taylor. What a pleasant surprise!
To what do I owe this pleasure?" she asked.

"I wanted to stop by and say thank you," said Taylor.
"I made some roasted pumpkin seeds just for you."

"How kind of you!" exclaimed Mrs. Squirrel.
"Happy Thanksgiving Taylor!"

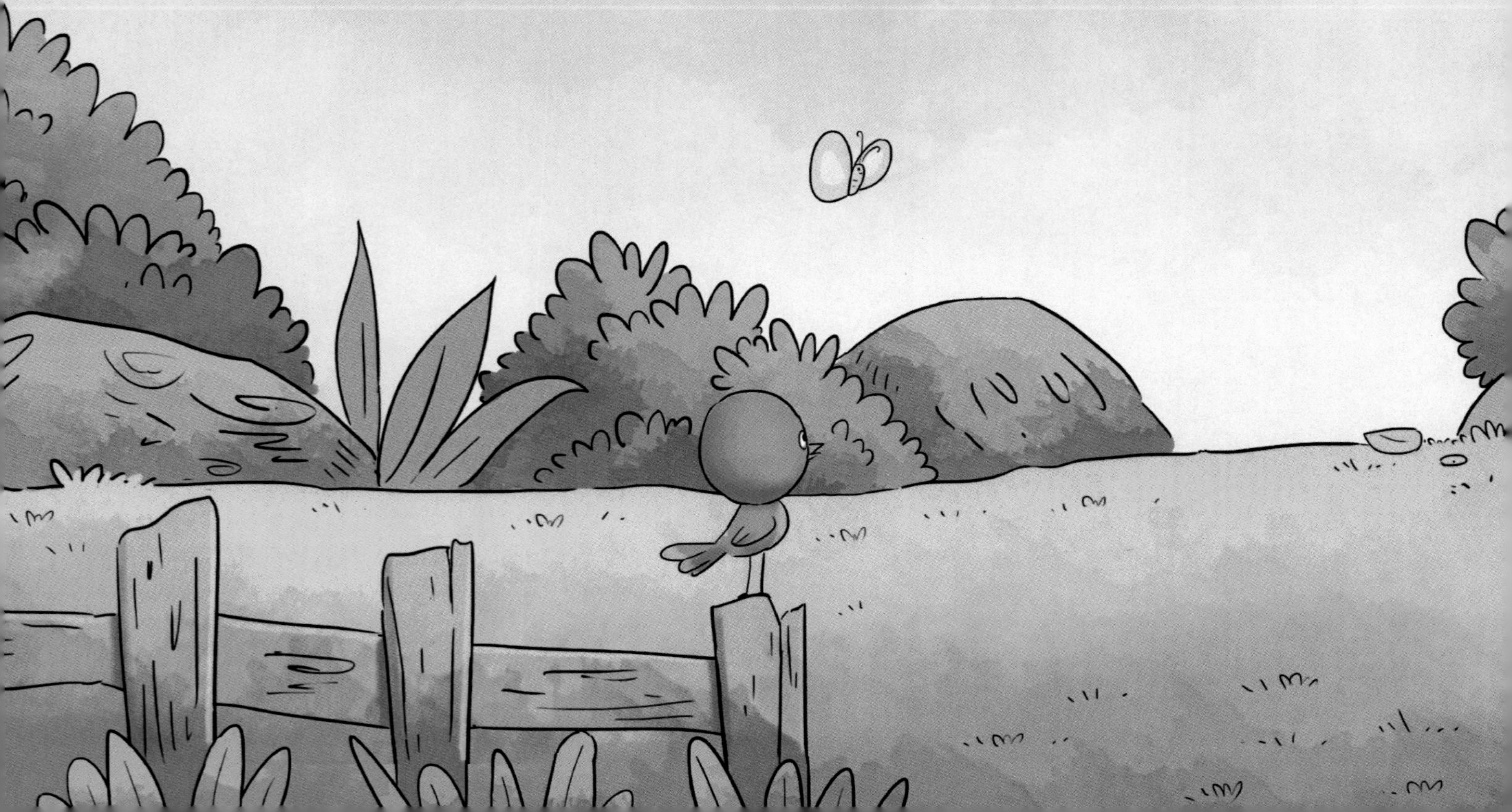

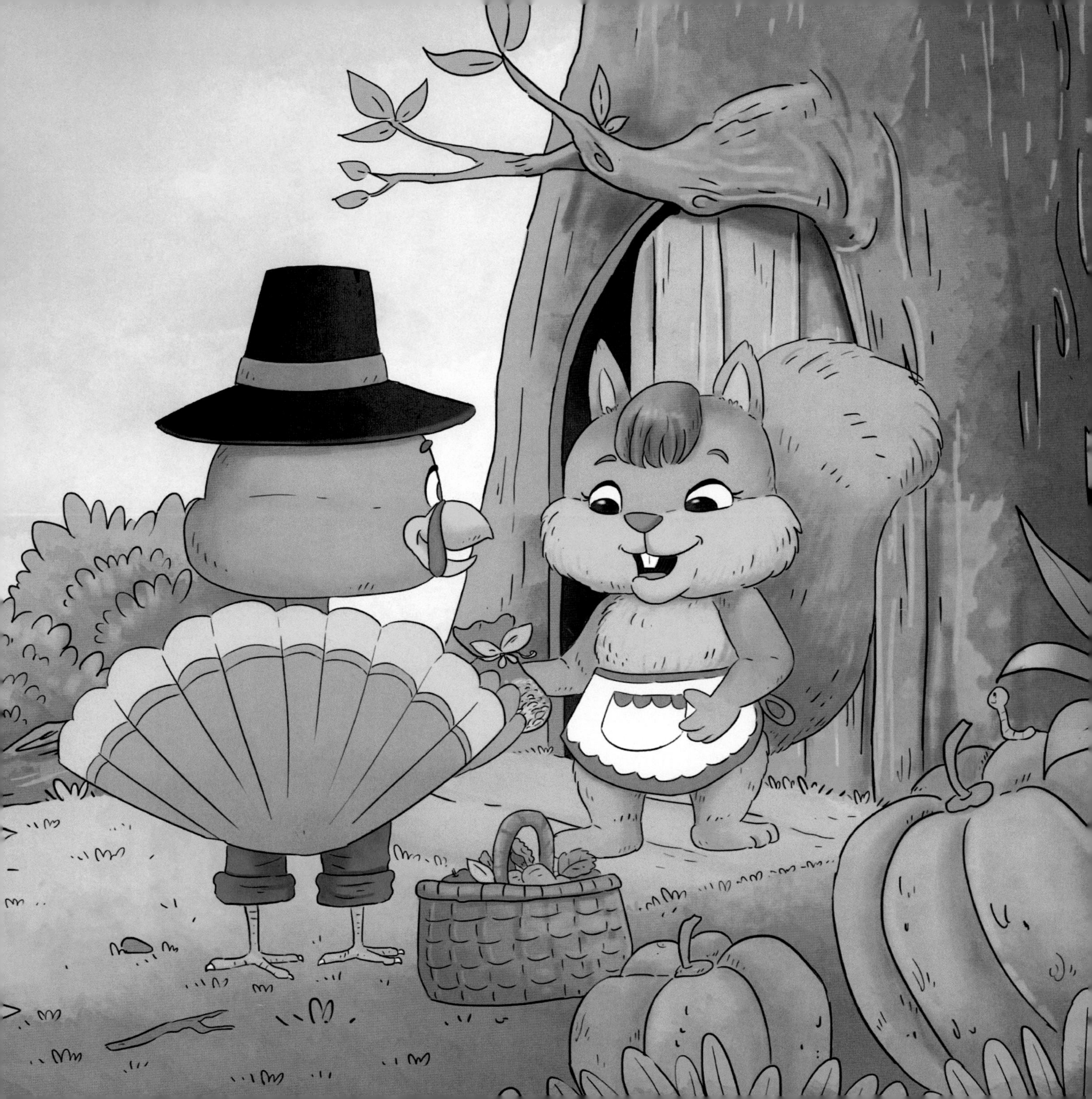

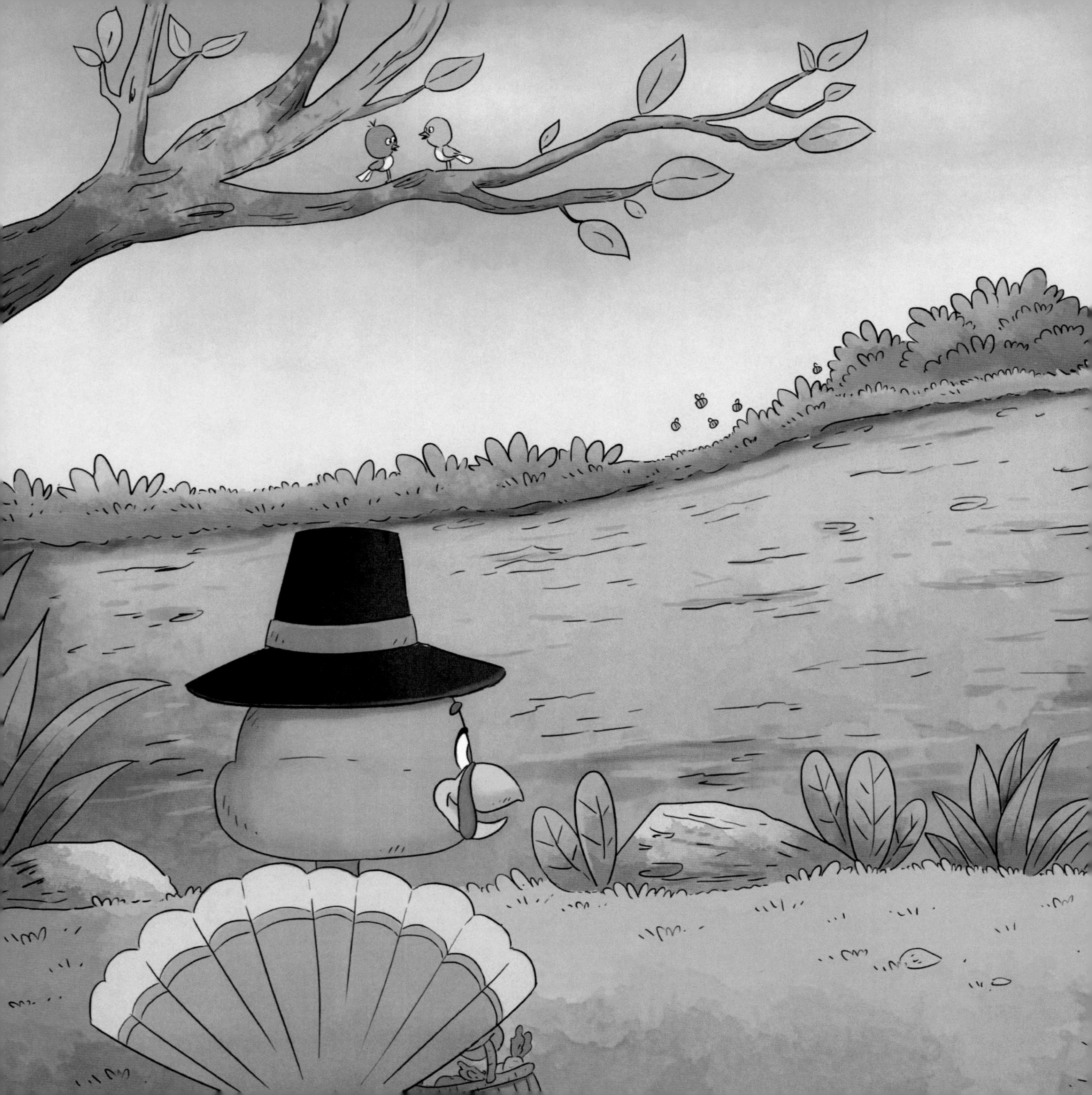

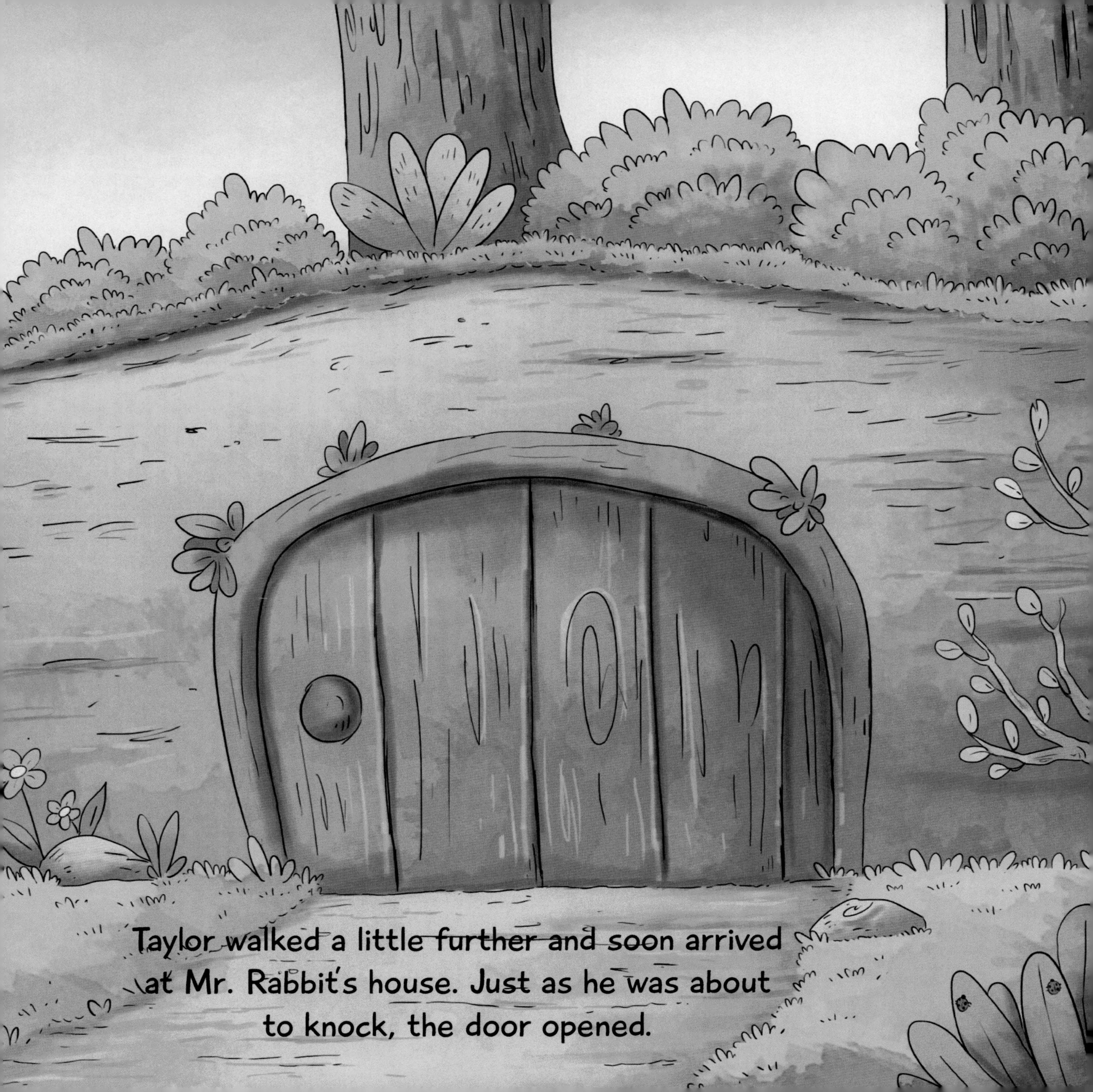

Taylor walked a little further and soon arrived at Mr. Rabbit's house. Just as he was about to knock, the door opened.

"Well, hello, Taylor. It's always nice to see you," said Mr. Rabbit.
"I wanted to stop by and give you this basket of carrots,"
said Taylor. "They're fresh from my garden.
Happy Thanksgiving Mr. Rabbit!"

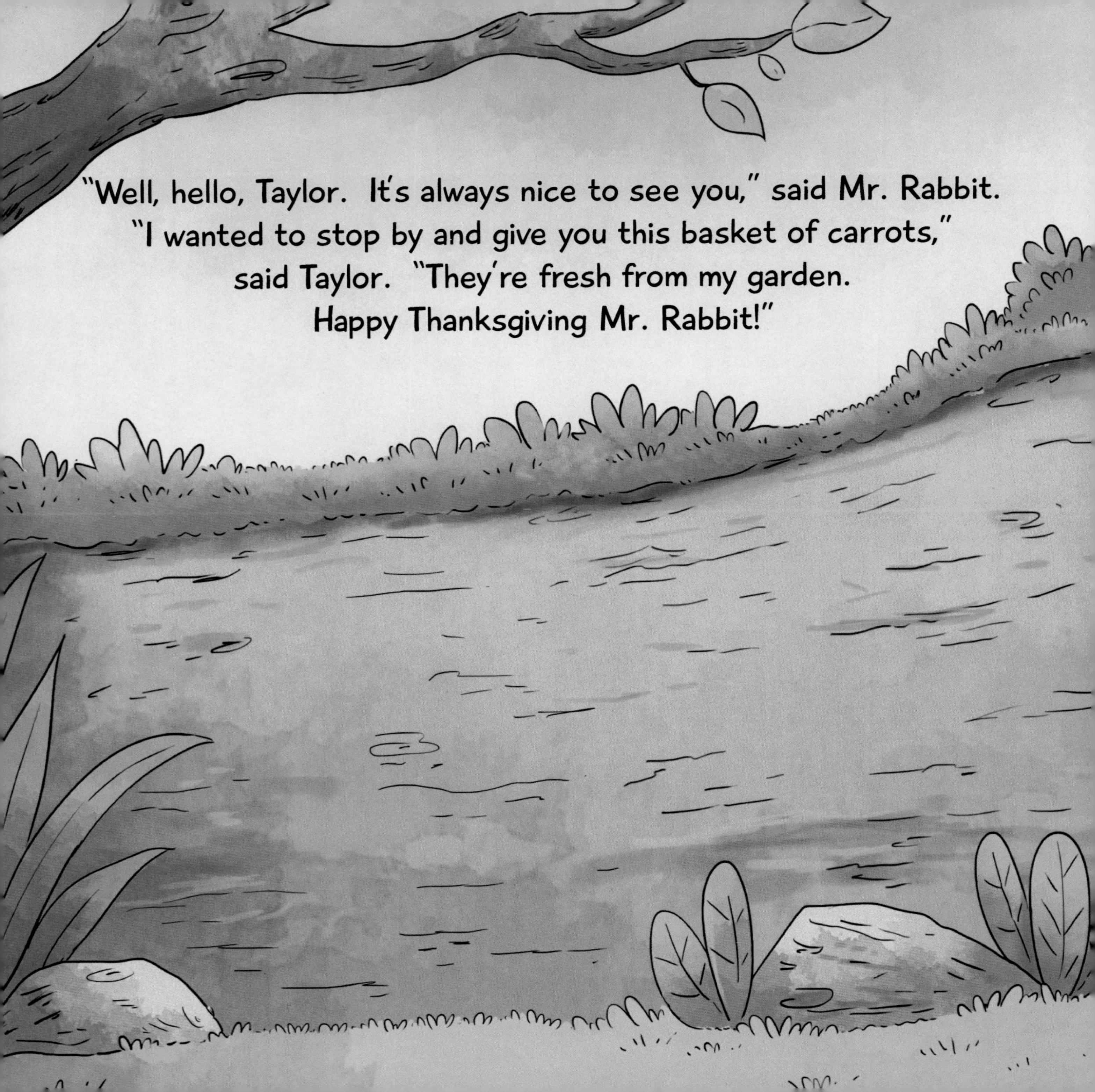

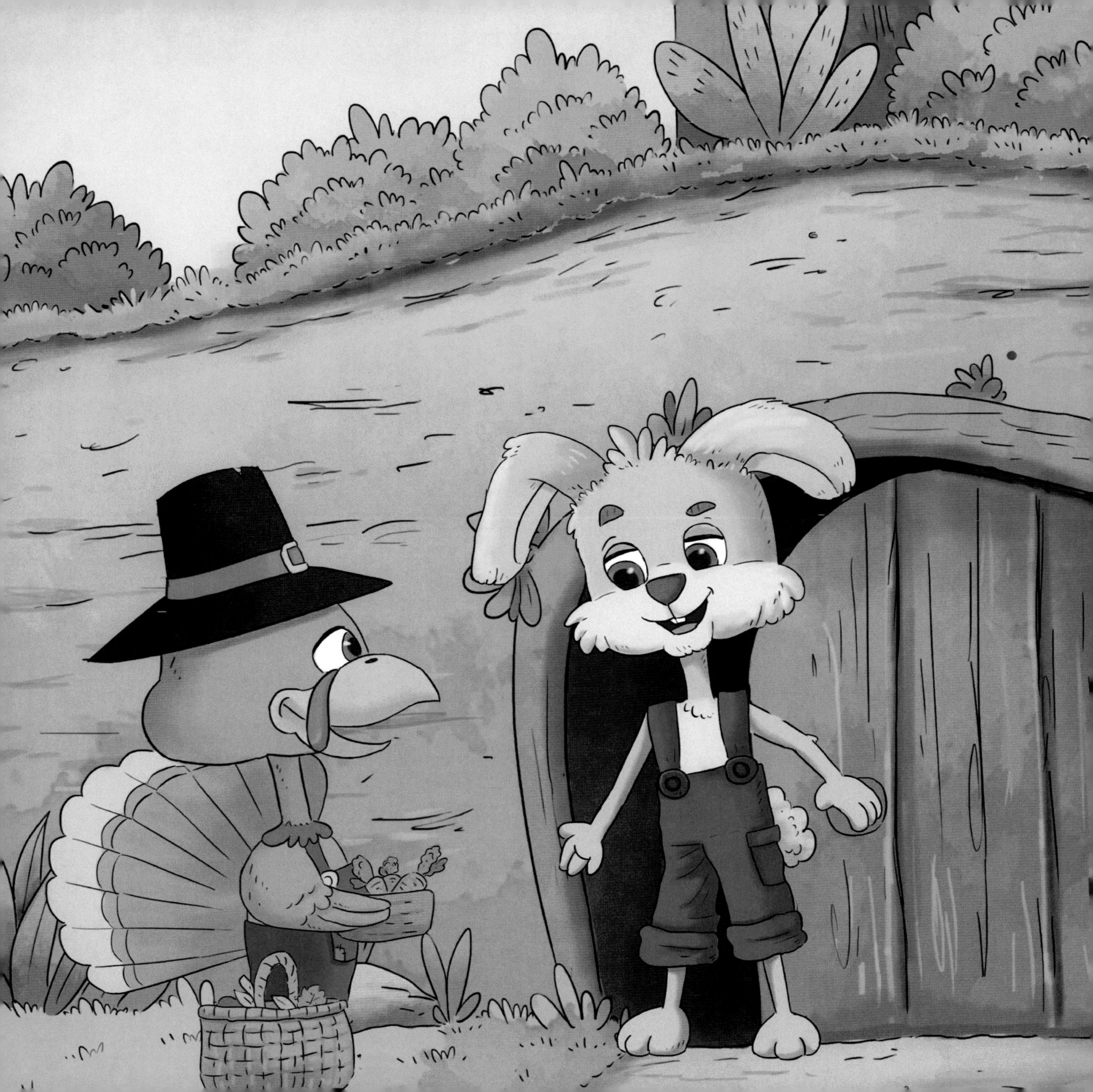

Taylor visited all his neighbors, family, and all his friends.
He told them how thankful he was to have them in his life,
and he gave each of them something from his garden.

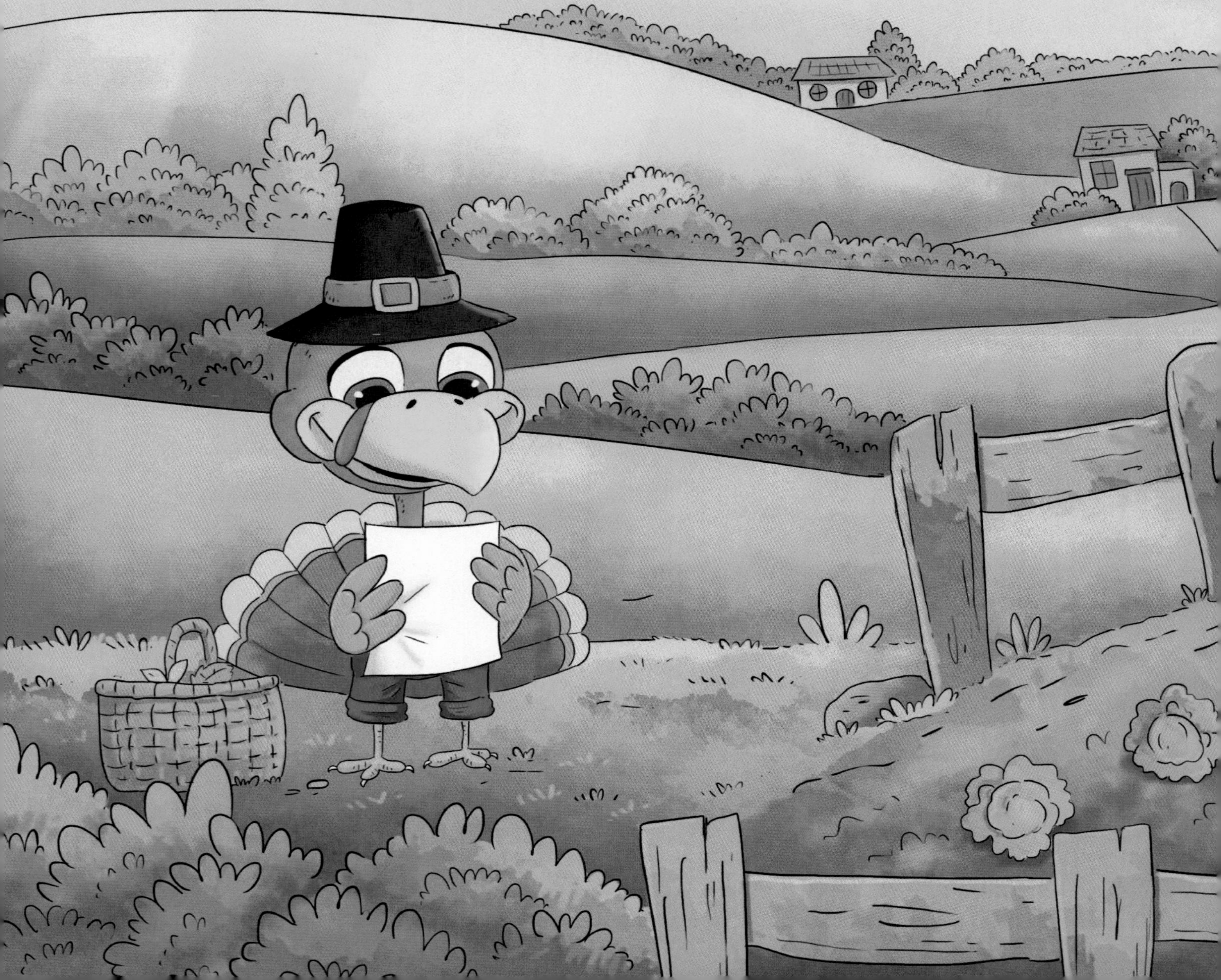

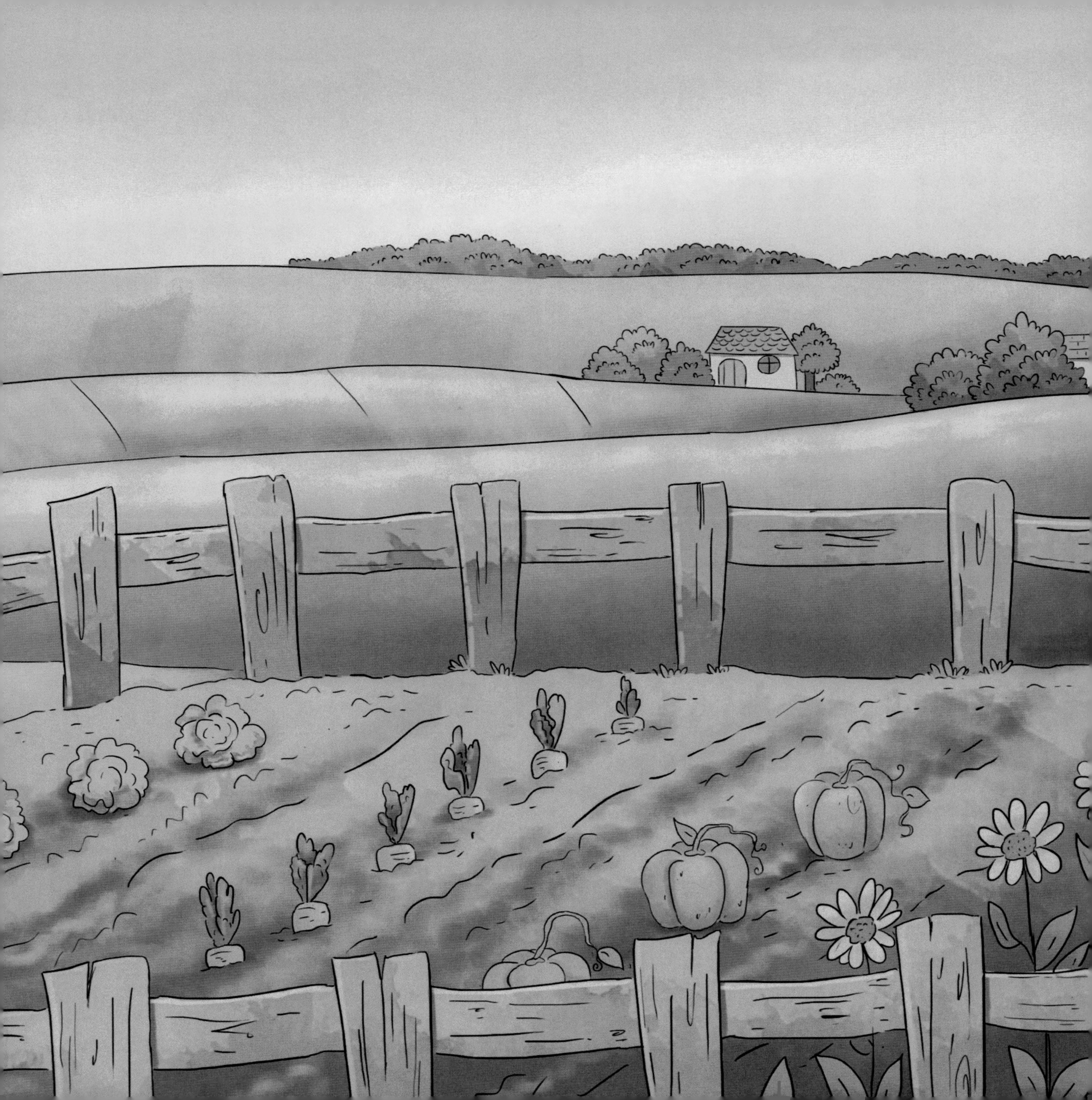

Before long, word of what Taylor had done spread through the town.
Everyone decided to follow in Taylor's footsteps.

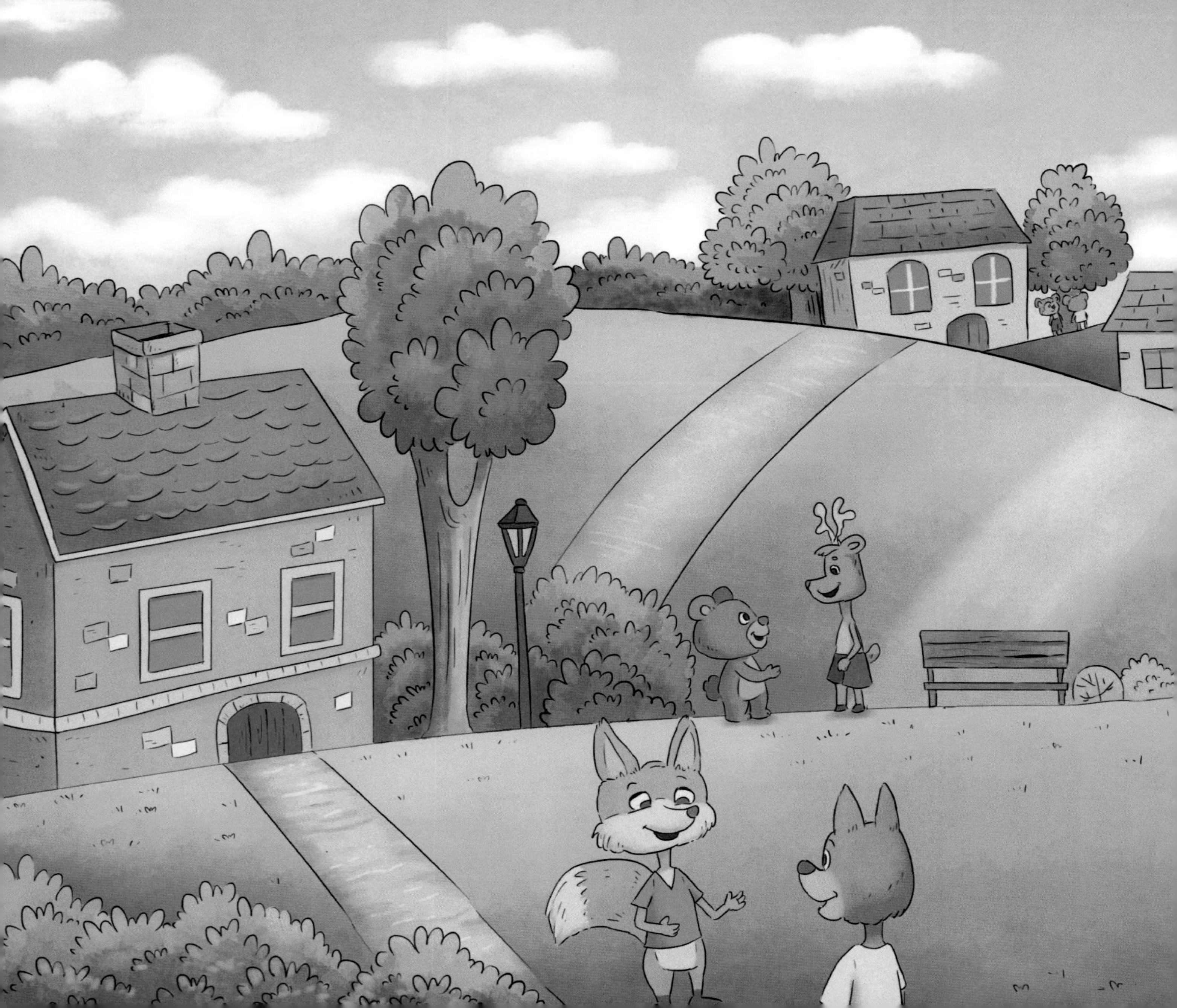

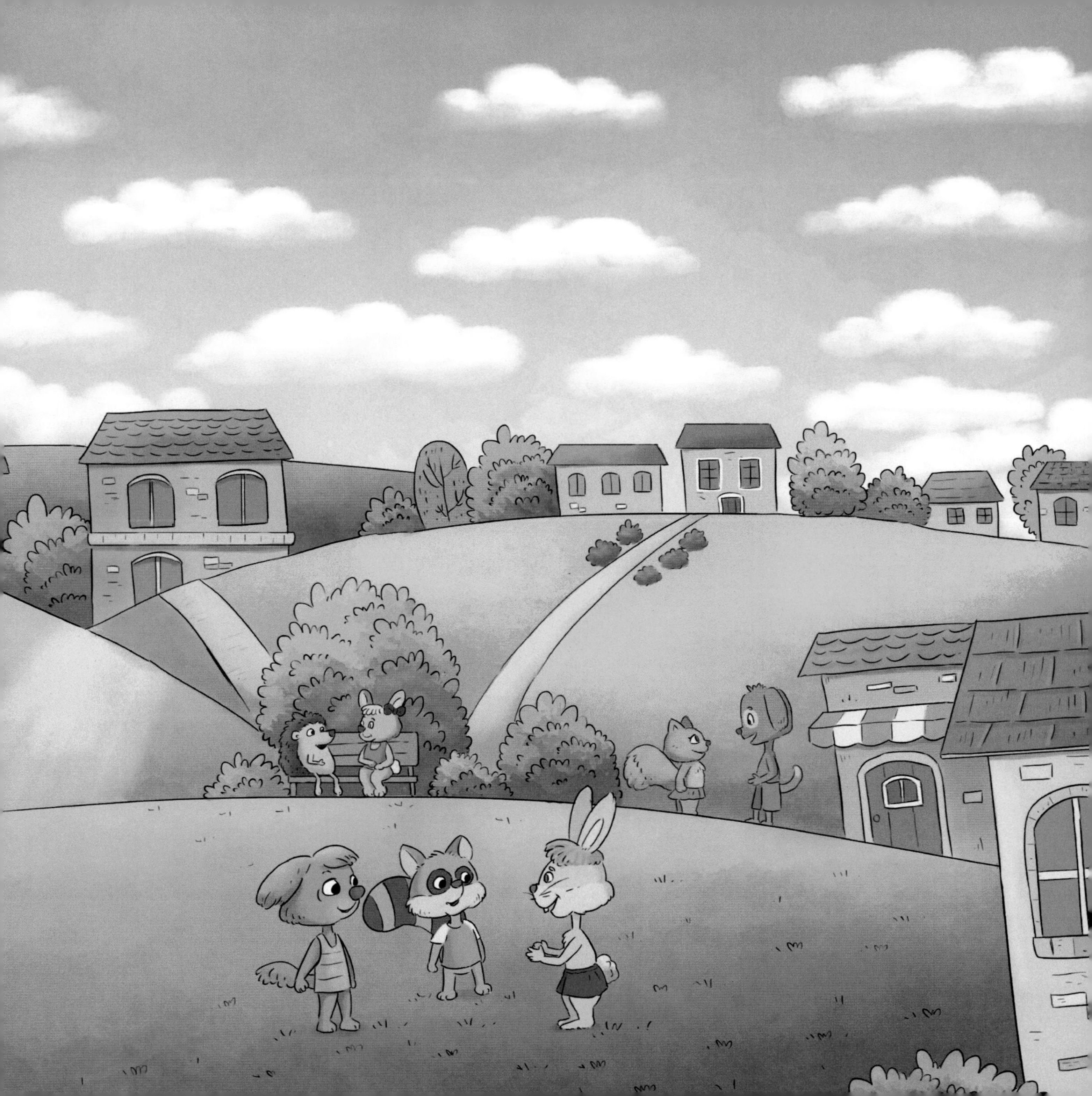

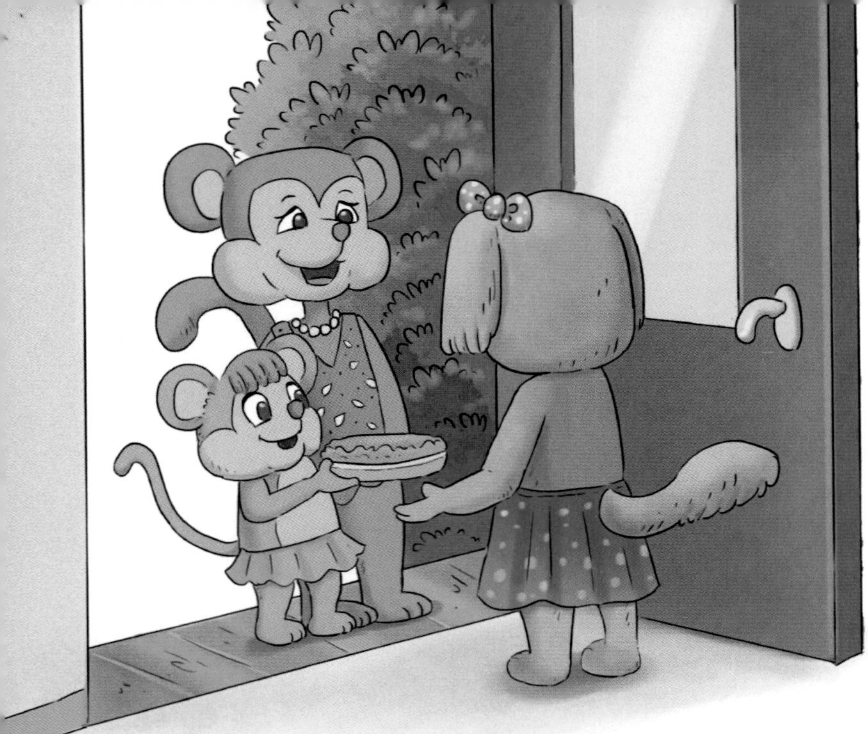

Gifts of sweet potato pie
and cranberry jams were
exchanged.

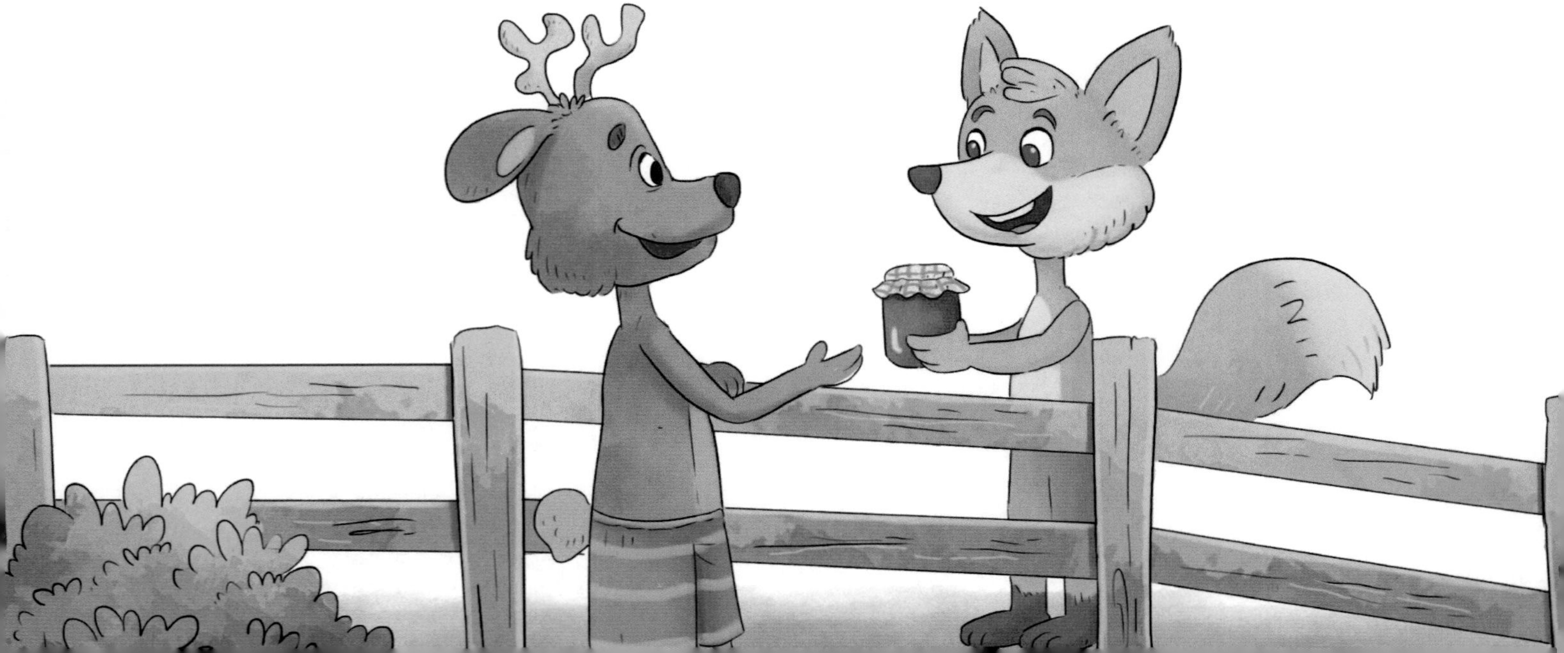

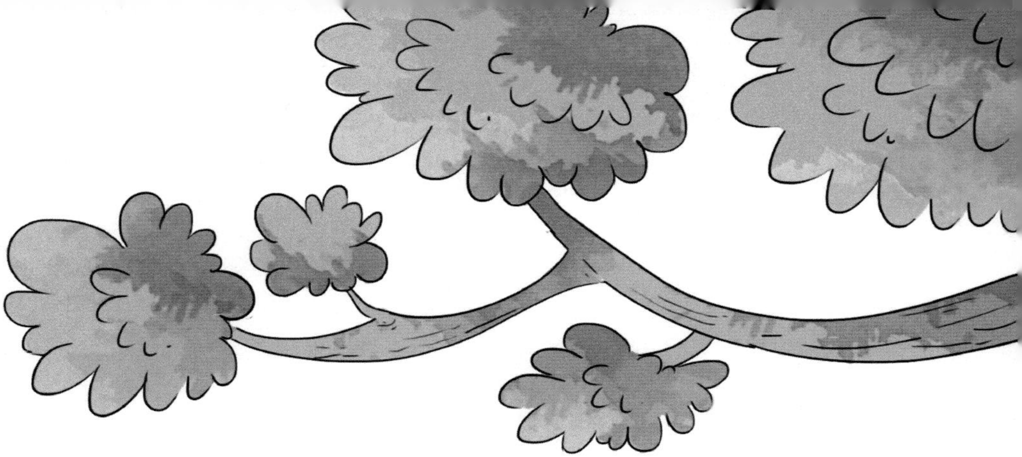

Letters and words of encouragement shared,
and the message was always the same...

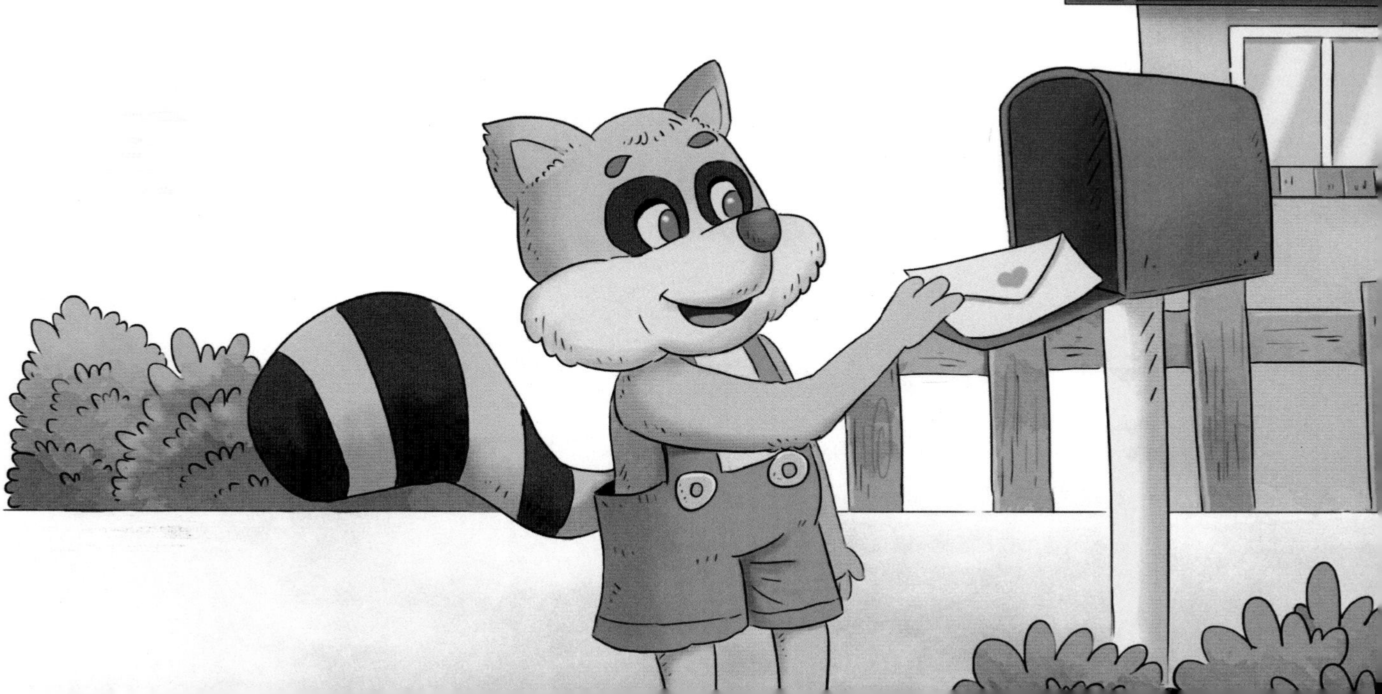

Big or small, always be thankful for what you have!

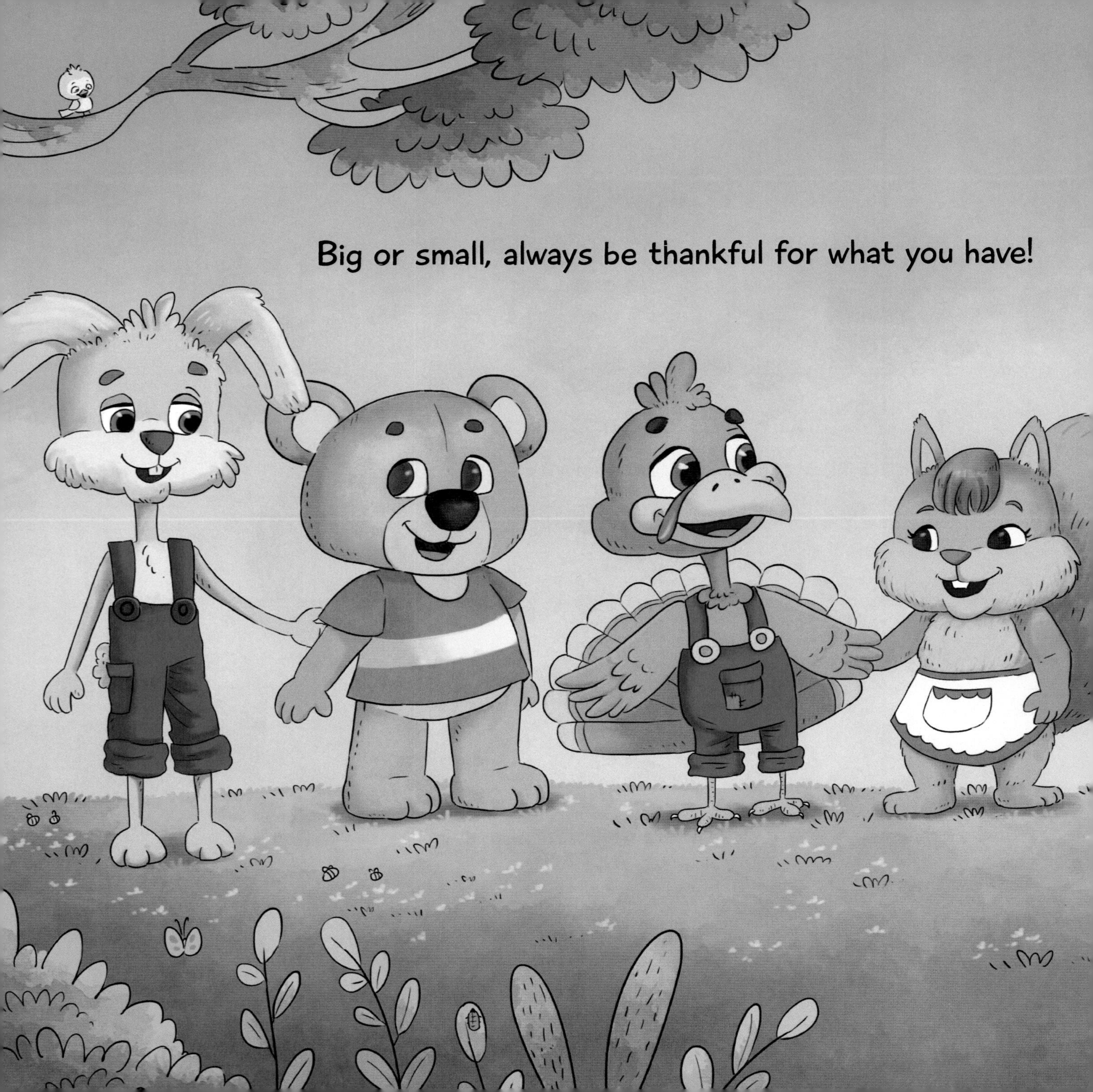

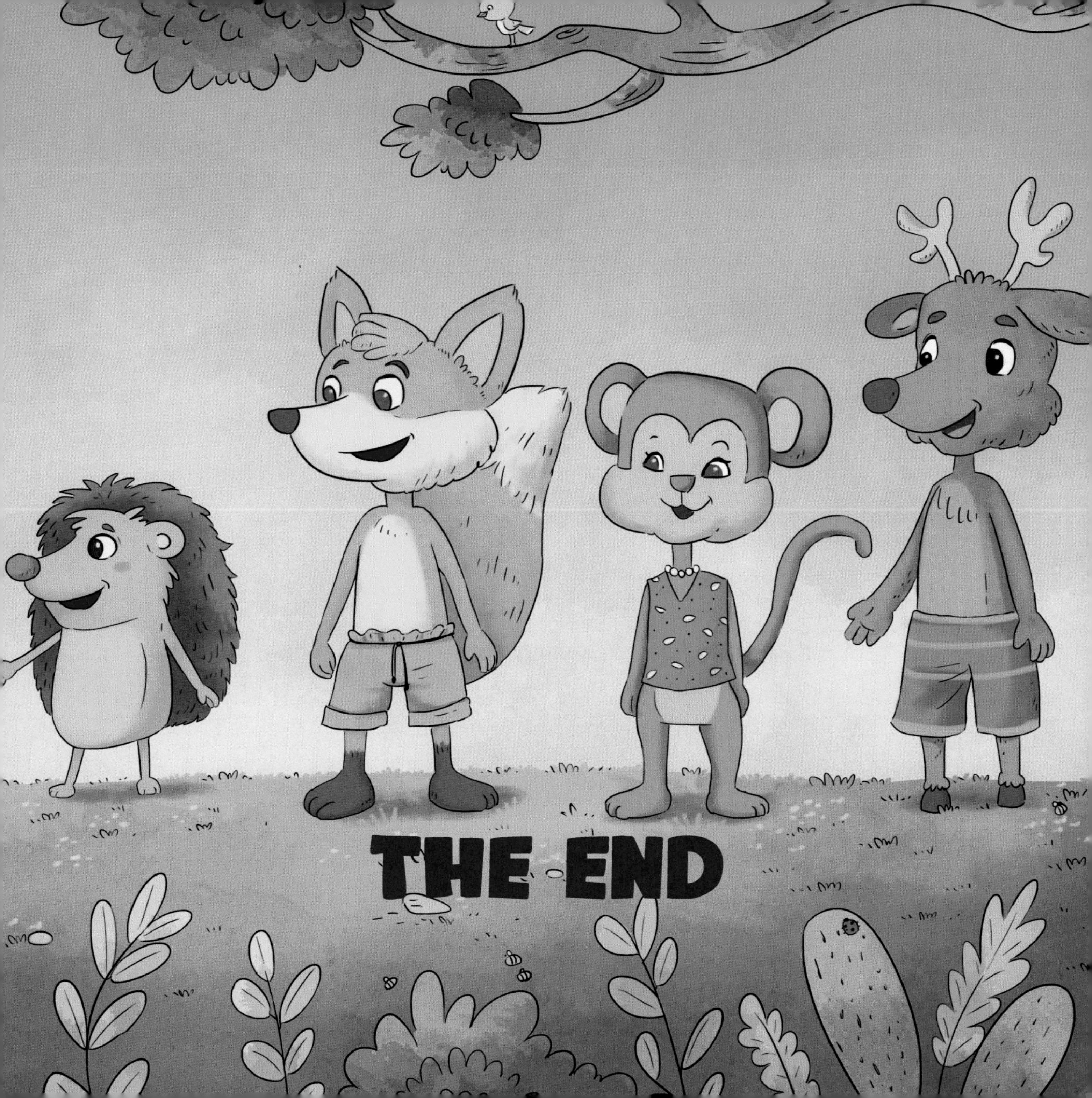
THE END

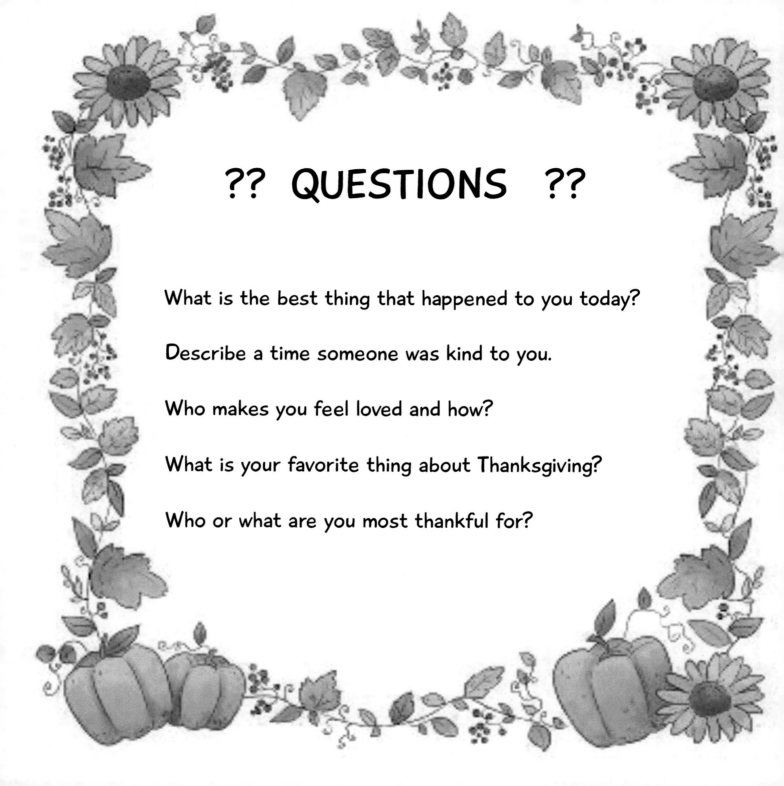

?? QUESTIONS ??

What is the best thing that happened to you today?

Describe a time someone was kind to you.

Who makes you feel loved and how?

What is your favorite thing about Thanksgiving?

Who or what are you most thankful for?

THANKSGIVING
SCAVENGER HUNT

- PUMPKIN
- RED APPLE
- TWIGS
- BERRIES
- SQUIRREL
- VEGETABLES
- YELLOW LEAF
- FOOTBALL
- PILGRIM HAT
- BLACK BIRD

- ACORN
- SCARECROW
- WISHBONE
- PUMPKIN PIE
- OWL
- FEATHER
- PINECONE
- SEEDS
- TURKEY
- FALL DECORATIONS

Place a check ✓ next to each item you find.
The first one to find all the items wins!

Made in the USA
Las Vegas, NV
19 November 2021

34829543R00017